THE LITTLE SEAHORSE RESCUE

written by Desirree Madison-Biggs
illustrated by Liliia Martyniuk

Copyright © 2024 Desirree Madison-Biggs

All rights reserved. This book or parts thereof may not be reproduced in any form, stored in any retrieval system, or transmitted in any form by any means—electronic, mechanical, photocopy, recording, or otherwise—without prior written permission of the publisher, except as provided by United States of America copyright law. For permission requests, write to the publisher.

This is a work of fiction. Names, characters, business, events and incidents are the products of the author's imagination. Any resemblance to actual persons, living or dead, or actual events is purely coincidental.

ISBN: 978-1-960157-61-4 (Paperback)
ISBN: 978-1-960157-62-1 (Hardcover)

The Little Seahorse Rescue

By Desirree Madison-Biggs

1. Fiction

FIRST EDITION

Illustrated by Liliia Martyniuk

Edited by John Fox

Published by Bookfox Press

Printed in the United States of America

To my daughter, Dylan, whose heart is as big as the sea
and to the compassionate and dedicated staff at the Waikiki Aquarium

Off the shimmering waters surrounding the lush island lived a community of seahorses. Each day as the sun rose, they would eat, swim, and sway together, holding on to the long sea grasses that grew in clumps at the sandy bottom.

There was one little seahorse who never wanted to let go of the sea grasses. Hanging on made him feel safe and protected.

One morning, dark clouds gathered, and a terrible storm erupted. Great winds whipped the waves above, which swayed the grasses below. The seahorse gripped the blade with his little tail as tightly as he could, but the current was too strong.

Tumbling head over tail, he was pulled to the surface and sucked back down over and over again.

After a time, the winds stopped, and the ocean calmed. Where was he? Nothing around him looked familiar. He looked everywhere for something to hang on to, but there was only emptiness.

All at once, a great force lifted him up, up, up, and then down onto the sandy shore with a whoosh. The brightness stunned him. This did not feel right at all, not one bit. Where were the cool waters and waving grasses of his home?

From overhead, a shadow loomed, and he felt himself rising into the air. A girl with worried green eyes peered down at him. She wondered what to do. The waves were too rough to put him back into the sea. Scooping him up, she trickled cool water over him.

Wait, he was moving again. Where was he going now?

Suddenly, he felt himself drifting down into water. He felt scared. Where could he hide? What could he hang on to so he wouldn't float away?

Fluttering his tiny fins as hard as he could, he swam around the bowl.

Seabiscuit noticed a new object next to him. It wasn't sea grass, but it had branches. He wrapped his tail tightly around it.

Several times a day, tiny shrimp dropped around him. He was hungry and they looked familiar but not good enough to eat. He longed for the swaying sea grasses of his home.

Two days went by and still Seabiscuit clung to his branch and would not eat. The girl grew worried. Would her new pet ever eat? As much as she wanted to keep him, she knew her little friend needed help.

She contacted the city aquarium and they came up with a solution.

They could provide a home and the right food, but it would be up to Seabiscuit to eat.

The girl felt sad. If they took him, Seabiscuit would no longer belong to her.
However, one look at the hungry little seahorse helped her make the decision.
There was no time to lose.

Soon after, Seabiscuit was carried carefully into the car. With the water sloshing, he hung on as they drove into the city.

When they arrived at the aquarium, they were greeted by a young man with curly brown hair. The way the wind blew his hair reminded Seabiscuit of the grasses of his home. This made him happy, and he fluttered his fins.

The girl didn't want to leave him.

What would happen to him? Would she ever see her little friend again?

Later the next day, the girl received a text from the young man that Seabiscuit had started eating! She felt happy and relieved. She had made the right decision.

Before long, Seabiscuit was strong enough to be moved to a new tank of his own. He was placed in the seahorse exhibit at the front of the aquarium where his special friend and visitors from all over the world could watch him gracefully float and gently sway while holding on to sea grasses that felt just like home.

What do you think?

- Should the girl have taken the seahorse home?

- Did the girl do the right thing giving Seabiscuit to the aquarium? Why do you think that?

- What animal would you most like to find?

- What would you do if you found a lost animal?

*Seabiscuit was one of the most remarkable and beloved Thoroughbred racehorses in history. Despite the fact that he was small and ungainly he become a champion.

About the Author

Desirree Madison-Biggs is a debut children's author who has always had a passion for storytelling and a dream to write for young readers. She is inspired by children's innate compassion for animals and curiosity about the natural world. When she's not writing, Desirree enjoys exploring the ever changing shores of her home, traveling, and collecting stories from the people she meets on her adventures. She lives in a cozy cottage by the beach with her young adult daughter. They are the guardians of four community cats, Pebbles, Sunny, Skye, and Misty.

About the Illustrator

Liliia Martyniuk is a Ukrainian children's book illustrator who creates bright and colorful art with traditional media such as watercolors and colored pencils. She has illustrated more than 30 kid's books including *Colors of Ukraine* by Camille Campbell and *Rucksack* by Di Redmond—a therapeutic book for and about Ukrainian refugee kids. Her illustrated books have been published in Ukraine, the USA, the UK, Ireland, Spain, and Poland.

Printed in the USA
CPSIA information can be obtained
at www.ICGtesting.com
LVHW060209200624
783476LV00008B/234